Hammerhead Sharks

by Nico Barnes

ABDO SHARKS Kids

Visit us at www.abdopublishing.com

Published by Abdo Kids, a division of ABDO, PO Box 398166, Minneapolis, Minnesota 55439.

Printed in China

032014

092014

THIS BOOK CONTAINS RECYCLED MATERIALS

Photo Credits: Getty Images, iStock, Shutterstock, Thinkstock

Production Contributors: Teddy Borth, Jennie Forsberg, Grace Hansen

Design Contributors: Dorothy Toth, Renée LaViolette, Laura Rask

Library of Congress Control Number: 2013952572

Cataloging-in-Publication Data

Barnes, Nico.

Hammerhead sharks / Nico Barnes.

p. cm. -- (Sharks)

ISBN 978-1-62970-066-3 (lib. bdg.)

Includes bibliographical references and index.

1. Hammerhead sharks--Juvenile literature. I. Title.

597.3--dc23

2013952572

Table of Contents

Hammerhead Sharks 4

Hunting 12

Food 16

Baby Hammerhead Sharks 18

More Facts 22

Glossary 23

Index 24

Abdo Kids Code. 24

Hammerhead Sharks

Hammerhead sharks are named for the **unusual** shape of their heads.

Hammerhead sharks **prefer** to live in warm ocean water. You will often find them near **coastlines**.

Most hammerhead sharks are greenish in color. Others are gray. They have white bellies.

A hammerhead shark's eyes are set on either side of its head. Its large **dorsal fins** are easy to spot.

Hunting

Hammerhead sharks are good hunters. They have **sensors** on their heads that help them **scan** for food.

A hammerhead shark's flat head helps it to hunt. It can trap its **prey** on the ocean floor.

Food

The hammerhead shark's favorite meal is a stingray. It also eats fish, octopus, and other sharks.

Baby Hammerhead Sharks

Hammerhead sharks give birth from 2 to 42 **pups** at a time.

Hammerhead shark **pups** have rounder heads. Their heads will **flatten** as they grow.

More Facts

- Hammerhead sharks can live for 20 to 30 years in the wild.
- There are around 9 different species of hammerhead sharks.
- Hammerhead sharks range in size depending on species. The smallest hammerhead shark, the scalloped bonnethead, is about 3 feet (.9 m) long. The largest, the great hammerhead, can grow to be 20 feet (6 m).

Glossary

coastline – where land and water meet.

dorsal fin – the tall, triangular fin of a shark.

flatten – to make flat.

prefer – like better than other options.

prey – an animal hunted or killed for food.

pup – a newborn animal.

scan – to look over to see something.

sensor – anything that can register physical features.

unusual – different, or unlike similar things.

Index

babies 18, 20

coloring 8

dorsal fin 10

eyes 10

food 12, 14, 16

habitat 6

head 4, 10, 12, 14, 20

hunting 12, 14

ocean 6, 14

sensors 12

abdokids.com

Use this code to log on to abdokids.com and access crafts, games, videos and more!